The Spy's Guide to Escape and Evasion

BY **HenaKhan**

WITH **H.KeithMelton**
SPY EXPERT

SCHOLASTIC INC.

NEW YORK   TORONTO   LONDON   AUCKLAND   SYDNEY
MEXICO CITY   NEW DELHI   HONG KONG   BUENOS AIRES

**When it's time to make an escape, a spy has
to have the right gear. This miniature telescope can be easily
carried in a pocket, and the escape map is made of fabric
instead of paper, so it can be unfolded quietly.**

ISBN 0-439-33648-1

Copyright © 2003 by Scholastic Inc.

Editor: Andrea Menotti
Designers: Robert Rath, Lee Kaplan
Illustrations: Daniel Aycock

Photos: Page 26, courtesy of the Moorland-Springarn Research Center.
All other photos: www.spyimages.net.

12 11 10 9 8 7   6 7 8/0

Printed in the U.S.A.

First Scholastic printing, June 2003

The publisher has made every effort to ensure that the activities in this book are safe when done as instructed.
Children are encouraged to do their spy activities with willing friends and family members and to respect others'
right to privacy. Adults should provide guidance and supervision whenever the activity requires.

TABLE OF Contents

👓 This means you'll use your Spy Gear in this activity.

💻 This means you can find a related activity on the Spy University web site.

On the

So, you've been working hard on your spy missions and learning about all kinds of spies throughout history. Are you ready for a pop quiz?

Who is the most successful spy of all time?

Don't know? Good—because that's the right answer! The *most* successful spies are the ones whom the rest of the world *never* finds out about. Instead of making big headlines, the best spies go quietly about their spy business, while everyone else (except their **handlers**, of course) is fooled into thinking they're just ordinary people.

The Most Successful Spy of All Time

Even if they help win a war, catch a terrorist, or alter the course of history, the best spies rarely get a taste of fame or even a share of the credit. But that's okay by them, because fame in the spy world usually comes at a high price...getting caught!

You've already learned how to keep your spy operations under wraps, which is the first step to being a successful spy. But what if something goes wrong? What if your secrets are exposed, and **counterspies** are hot on your trail? That's when you need to know the **tradecraft** of escape and **evasion** (or E & E, as spies call it). This month's guide will teach you the techniques and strategies you need to make super-speedy getaways when counterspies are closing in.

Spy Caught Red-Handed!

Evasion:
Steps taken to avoid capture or other dangers

But don't make a run for it yet! First we need to *catch* you up on a few escape and evasion basics.

F:RUN!

WHEN DO SPIES NEED TO ESCAPE?

As you know, the world of spies is all about secrets—finding secrets, keeping secrets, and living a secret life. When a spy's secrets get out, the spy needs to get *away*. Maybe a mission went wrong, maybe the spy was turned in by another spy, or maybe he just made a simple error in tradecraft.

Whatever the reason, an exposed spy needs to get away before he's put under heavy **surveillance**, held for questioning, or even imprisoned. If the spy manages to escape, he has a chance to continue his spy career under a new **cover**. If not, he could end up in the Spy Hall of *Shame*!

WHAT GOES INTO A SUCCESSFUL ESCAPE?

When it comes to escape and evasion, spies need to remember three things:

■ **Be prepared.** Since you never know when you might need to make a quick getaway, it's important to be ready at all times with an escape plan and essential getaway goods.

■ **Have the right stuff.** The right gear can make the difference between escape and capture.

This escape kit from World War II (1939–1945) contains a silk map (that opens quietly, without loud rustling that would attract attention), a photo that can be used to make a fake ID card, a compass to help the escapee find his way, and a saw blade that can cut through metal chains or fences.

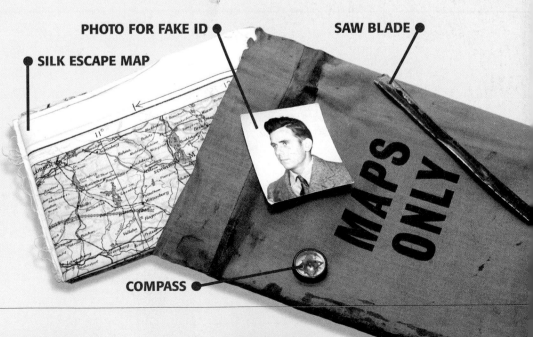

PHOTO FOR FAKE ID ●

SAW BLADE ●

● SILK ESCAPE MAP

MAPS ONLY

COMPASS ●

■ **Use your spy know-how.** This is when your spy skills and smarts can really save the day! You already learned one smart escape tactic in your *Trainee Handbook*: the quick-change, in which you slip on a hat or new jacket to throw someone off your trail. Escaping spies also need to know how to move secretly in the dark, how to navigate through unknown territory with a compass, and how to signal for help with flashes of light (see page 16) or taps on a wall (see page 42)!

Above all else, spies need courage and a lot of luck to escape. We can't help you out in the courage department (and we don't need to, right?). But we *can* wish you plenty of luck (which, hopefully, you'll never need!) and set you up with a new round of escape and evasion operations that'll get you prepared to make a speedy exit—should ever the need arise!

ABOUT THIS MONTH'S SPY GEAR

We're *breaking out* some of our most helpful escape-related Spy Gear this month! You've been issued:

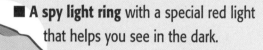

■ **A glow-in-the-dark compass** to help you find your way to safety from wherever you are!

■ **A spy light ring** with a special red light that helps you see in the dark.

■ **A signal mirror** so you can call for help with flashes of light.

ABOUT THIS MONTH'S WEB SITE

Don't let a chance to test your escape and evasion skills *get away* from you! Make your way to the Spy University web site at **www.scholastic.com/spy** to practice your new tradecraft. Remember to bring along this month's password!

the **password** spot

Shhhh.
This month's
web site password is
getaway

SPY TALK

▼ **Bearing:** The direction you have to head to reach a particular location.

▼ **Bug-out kit:** A collection of essential items for use during escape and evasion (including an escape map, a compass, emergency food, and other items).

▼ **Cache:** A secure place to hide things. (Pronounced "cash.")

▼ **Camouflage:** To disguise something by making it blend with its surroundings.

▼ **Code:** A system designed to hide the meaning of a message by substituting letters, numbers, words, symbols, sounds, or signals in place of the actual text.

▼ **Concealment:** An object that has been altered for the secret storage of messages, film, a camera, or other spy supplies.

▼ **Counterspy:** Someone who works in counterintelligence, investigating and catching spies.

▼ **Cover:** A false identity or a business that spies use as a front to conceal their espionage.

▼ **Danger signal:** A prearranged code used by a spy to alert his handlers that he has been captured or that he is at risk of capture. A danger signal can also be sent by the handler to warn the spy.

▼ **Dead drop:** A secure hiding place used for secret exchanges between a spy and a handler.

▼ **Decoy:** Something used to fool, lure, or draw attention toward one thing and away from another.

▼ **Defect:** To leave the control of a country or intelligence service to serve another country.

▼ **Evasion:** Steps taken to avoid capture or other dangers.

▼ **Handler:** The intelligence officer who manages an agent and gives him assignments.

▼ **Landmark:** An obvious object or place used as a reference to help a spy locate something.

▼ **Mole:** An employee of an intelligence service who secretly works for another country's intelligence service.

▼ **Safe house:** A place where members of a spy network can meet without worrying about being seen or heard by counterspies.

▼ **Spy network:** A group of spies who work together toward a common goal.

▼ **Surveillance:** The careful study and observation of someone or something.

▼ **Tradecraft:** The special techniques and procedures spies use to do their work.

A word to wise spies

- When planning your escape routes, limit them to familiar and safe places (no trespassing on private property!), and practice them with friends and family.

- Ask a senior spy to join you on your operations anytime you venture outdoors after nightfall. Don't be in the *dark* when it comes to safety!

 See how well you know your Spy Talk by playing a round of Spy Talk Hangman on the Spy University web site (www.scholastic.com/spy)!

The PAPER Chase

SPYquest

It's almost the end of the school day. You know you really *should* be concentrating on what your teacher is saying, but you just can't help watching the clock hands move closer to three o'clock. You're expecting an important secret message with details about an upcoming spy operation after school today. Finally, three o'clock arrives, the bell rings, and you rush out the doors. You head over to the park to your dead drop, where your secret message should be waiting.

Once you're at the park, you scan the area to make sure no one is around. Then you head toward a small group of trees and bushes behind the soccer field. You go straight to the second bush from the left—your spy network's agreed-upon dead drop location. Suddenly, you hear footsteps approaching. It's probably someone looking for a lost soccer ball, but you don't want to risk being seen, so you duck behind a tree and stay very still until the person walks by. After a minute, you peek out and see that…oh, no! It's not a soccer player after all, but that annoying school newspaper reporter, Justin, who's always into *everyone's* business.

A couple of days ago, Justin caught you as you were leaving science class and said he wanted to interview you for an upcoming cover story. He said he'd received a tip about some mysterious business that he wanted to investigate. You told him that you were really busy with your homework and that you didn't have time this week, hoping he would lose interest. Justin's always been a little too nosy for his own good, and you've been worried that he would try to find out about your spy activities. Now it looks like that's *exactly* what he's doing! Could he know something that's making him determined enough to follow you, even after you said you didn't have time to talk?

You don't want to risk uncovering the dead drop while Justin is snooping around. You can either just come back tomorrow when the coast should be clear, or you can follow Justin now to see if you can find out what he knows.

- If you decide to come back tomorrow, turn to **page 29**.
- If you decide to follow Justin to find out what he knows, turn to **page 27**.

This is your Spy Quest for this month. Choose your path wisely! If you hit a dead end, you'll have to back up and choose another path!

1

OPERATION Great ESCAPE

Your **cover** has been blown! Soon **counterspies** will be crawling all over your headquarters, and you *certainly* don't want to be there when they arrive. But where should you go? And how should you get there? There's no time to think these things through now. But don't panic! You've got an escape plan that has all the details you need to quickly get to a safe place, right? Not yet? Well then, you'd better grab your sneakers and *run*…through this operation!

STUFF YOU'LL NEED
• **Pencil and paper**
• **Colored pencils or markers**

YOUR NETWORK
• **Members of your spy network**

WHAT YOU DO

PART 1: MAP QUEST

In this part of the operation, you'll choose an escape route to a **safe house** (a meeting place where your **spy network** can safely gather). See if you've got the right instincts to get to safety!

1 First, study the map on the right. Your challenge is to get from your headquarters to the safe house without getting caught by counterspies who are on your trail. Do you see any areas you would want to avoid during your escape?

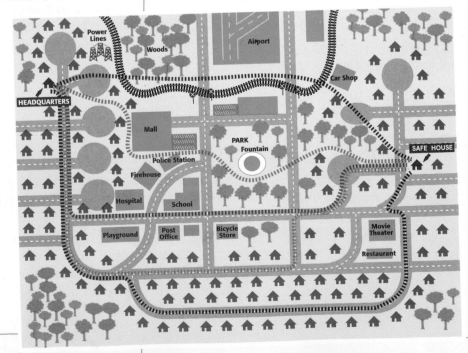

2 Now decide on the best route to the safe house. Consider each of the routes shown, and decide which one would present you with the fewest obstacles. Look out for things like:

- Long, winding routes that would take too much time.

- Crowded areas where you might be spotted by counterspies or witnesses who could help counterspies locate you later.

- Dangerous or prohibited areas.

3 Did you choose the wisest route to the safe house? Check out **What's the Secret** to find out!

PART 2: ESCAPE ARTIST

Now it's time to apply what you've learned to draw up your own escape plan.

1 Plan a secret meeting with your spy network to work out an escape plan for each member.

2 First, decide on a safe house. It should be a familiar place (like a friend's house) where the members of your spy network can secretly meet or hide.

3 Now pull out your pencil and paper and draw a map of your neighborhood. Start off by drawing your headquarters, the headquarters of the members of your spy network, and your safe house. Then add major **landmarks** (like signs, parks, and woods) and any potential obstacles (like watch dogs, security fences, and nosy neighbors!).

4 Brainstorm the best escape routes to get from each person's headquarters to the safe house. Keep the following tips in mind:

- The best route may not be the shortest or quickest way.

- You need to think about where you would be most likely to be spotted or heard by counterspies during your escape.

- It's a good idea to build options into your routes whenever you can, just in case you suddenly realize that you're being followed or that there is danger ahead.

5 Draw the routes on your map with the colored pencils or markers, using a different colored line for each route.

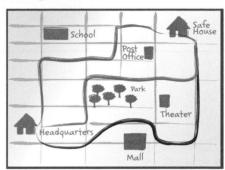

6 Practice "escaping" through the routes you've chosen with your spy network. That way, you'll be familiar with them in case you really need them!

WHAT'S THE SECRET?

Do you feel confident that you picked the best escape route in **Part 1**? Let's see how you did!

- If you picked the red escape route: Bad news! This route is the most dangerous, even though it's tempting since it's the shortest one. You'd pass by power lines (yikes!) and cross over railroad tracks (never!). Go back and carefully rethink your logic if this is the route you selected.

- If you picked the green escape route: Not the best choice! This route takes you through several busy areas including the mall and the park.

- If you picked the blue escape route: Think again! Like the green route, this path takes you through too many areas where you could be seen.

- If you picked the `orange` escape route: Good for you! This is the best bet. It takes you through no dangerous or prohibited areas, and it doesn't pass by any places where you'd have high chances of being spotted or stopped. Even though it's not the shortest route, it's the best choice.

- If you picked the `purple` route: You must have extra time on your hands! This is certainly a safe route, but it's way too long. The yellow route is a lot quicker.

Spies need to be able to think on their feet *and* use them quickly if they want to increase their chances of a safe escape. When faced with danger, it's common for people to panic or get confused, which adds to their risk. That's why a detailed escape plan can save the day. It's important to make sure that the plan is put down on paper, that it's easy to follow, and that you've practiced the different routes so you know them well.

MORE FROM HEADQUARTERS

It's just as important to have escape plans in your everyday life as it is in the spy world. Make sure your family is ready to act together quickly in case of an emergency. For example, if you don't already have a fire evacuation plan in place, set up a family meeting. Agree on a safe meeting place where everyone can gather outside your home after they've evacuated. Then draw a map of your home, and plan escape routes from each room. Think of more than one exit from each room in case the regular exit is blocked by flames or smoke. Practice the escape routes with your family, and review the map occasionally to keep your memory fresh.

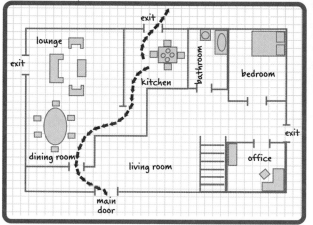

(*continued from page 27 or 29*)

You decide to set up a meeting with Spy Force One for the next morning before school to discuss the problem of Justin following you.

As you're leaving for the meeting the next morning, you see Justin waiting for you outside your house. This problem is even more serious than you thought! You have to leave by the back door in order to get to the meeting without Justin seeing you.

When everyone has arrived at the meeting, you tell your network about Justin. Sure enough, Liz says that she also had someone from the school newspaper trying to ask her questions before she gave him the slip. It seems like the newspaper crew will stop at nothing to get their story, and they'll be watching you pretty closely. It'll be trickier than ever to carry out your spy activities without being observed.

Sam suggests that it might be a good idea to do all your spy activities at night for a while, when they'll be less likely to be noticed. Zoe thinks that it might be a good idea to use a decoy the next time Justin is waiting for you outside your house so you can unload the dead drop without him following you.

- If you decide to do all your spy activities at night, turn to **page 15**.

- If you decide to use a decoy, turn to **page 37**.

2

OPERATION NIGHT Light

If you could choose the timing of your escape, wouldn't you make it during the night—when you could move under the cover of darkness? Good thinking. But while it's more difficult for **counterspies** to spot an escaping spy at night, it's just as tricky for *spies* to make their way without using an attention-grabbing flashlight. So what's the perfect escape tool in these situations? A spy light ring!

STUFF YOU'LL NEED

- **Escape items (like a compass or a watch)**
- **Pencil and paper**
- **Spy light ring**
- **Flashlight**

YOUR NETWORK

- **A friend to hide escape items**
- **A senior spy to be with you outside after dark**

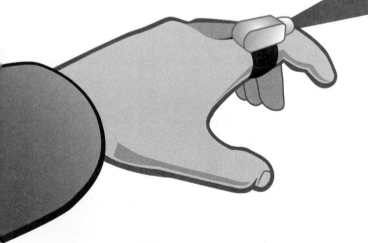

Your spy light ring can brighten your way with just enough red light to guide you. Plus, it sits on your finger, leaving your hands free to open doors, climb walls, or whatever else you need to do during your getaway. Slip on your light ring and see how it's just right for spying by night!

WHAT YOU DO

Note: This operation needs to take place outside on a clear night.

1 Look for a spot outside that gets pretty dark at night (somewhere away from bright streetlights). Make sure a senior spy joins you.

2 Have a friend hide five small escape items (like a compass, a watch, a rope, a signal mirror, and a map) in the area you've chosen. The items can be hidden under a bush or behind a tree, but they cannot be buried.

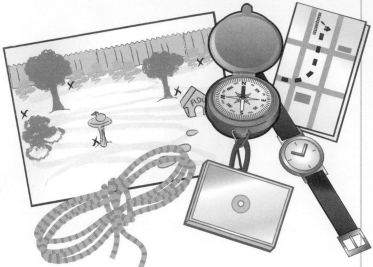

3 Your friend should then draw a map of the area for you, with marks that indicate where to find the hidden items.

4 After nightfall, take the map, put on your spy light ring, and go to the area where the items are hidden. Wait until your eyes adjust to the darkness so you can see well enough to move around comfortably.

5 First, try to find one of the items without using your spy light ring. Can you do it? How long does it take you?

6 Now turn on your spy light ring and use it to read the map. Turn off the light as soon as you're done reading the map.

7 Try to find the remaining hidden items, using the light ring only to read the map. After you turn off the light ring, do your eyes need to readjust to the dark, or can you find your way to the hidden items right away?

8 Try using a regular (white) flashlight to read the map. What do you notice when you turn off the light? How is your night vision?

MORE FROM HEADQUARTERS

If you need to write in the dark, try strapping your spy light ring to a pen or pencil!

WHAT'S THE SECRET?

What happens when someone turns on a bright light while you're sleeping in a dark room? Ouch! It certainly gets your attention (and hurts!), right? This is because the opening to your eye, the pupil, is adjusted by the iris (the colored part of your eye), which opens and closes depending on the amount of light in the room. When it's dark, the iris opens wide to let any amount of light in. If a light is suddenly turned on, the iris quickly closes, protecting your eye.

During an escape, it's better not to have to worry about letting your eyes adjust to drastic changes in light. Red light is the best color to use at night because it doesn't close your irises like white light does—they remain more open, so your night vision won't be impaired. That's why cars and airplanes often use red lights on their instrument panels. Stargazers also use red bulbs in their flashlights, or they cover the lenses with red cellophane, so that their night vision isn't affected when they have to look at their star charts or take notes. Your spy light ring helps you work in the dark better than a regular flashlight for the same reason.

PUPIL

IRIS

SPYquest

(continued from page 12)

You agree that it's a good idea to perform all of your spy operations under the cover of darkness, when it's less likely that reporters will be following you around. Plus, it'll give you a chance to use your cool spy light ring!

That night, you decide to retrieve your secret message. You're heading to the park after dinner and homework, when you notice a car is following you and staying right behind you. Just when you're starting to get nervous, you turn around and see that it's Dad in his car, wearing his bathrobe and a very angry expression.

"Where do you think you're going at this hour?" he demands. "Do you know what time it is, and how dangerous it is for you to be out alone? Get in this car right now!"

Oops! You should've made sure to run your idea by the senior spies. They probably would've pointed out that it wasn't the best one in the book. Now you're grounded, so no more spy activities for you for a while, day or night!

■ This was a dead end. Turn back and try again!

Light SAVER

#3

Phew! You managed to evade **counterspies** and get to a hiding place where they won't find you, at least for now. You're exhausted, but there's no time to relax. You need to find a way to get out of the area *completely*. Lucky for you, help is not far away.

This signal mirror was used during World War II (1939–1945).

Someone from your **spy network** will come pick you up and get you to a safe place once you send out the right signal. You don't have a cell phone, a pager, or a communication radio with you...so how are you going to get the message out? Check out how your signal mirror can get you help in a *flash*!

WHAT YOU DO

1 Go outside and have a friend stand 25 feet (7.5 m) away from you in the direction of the sun.

2 Holding your signal mirror in one hand, reflect light onto your other hand.

3 Slowly move the mirror toward your eye, making sure to keep the reflection on your other hand. When the mirror reaches your eye, look through the circle in the center at the light on your hand. You should see a bright spot of light, which will help you aim your signal.

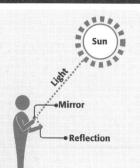

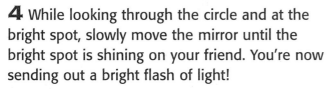

BRIGHT SPOT FOR AIMING SIGNAL

4 While looking through the circle and at the bright spot, slowly move the mirror until the bright spot is shining on your friend. You're now sending out a bright flash of light!

5 Wiggle the mirror from side to side to send out a repeating flash. Ask your friend to call out when he sees the flashes.

6 Take turns so that you both get a chance to send out and see the signals.

MORE FROM HEADQUARTERS

1 Try using other items as signal mirrors, such as CDs, pocket mirrors, or other shiny objects. Test to see how well these items work for signaling purposes. Have a friend stand far enough away from you that you do not see each other (but make sure that your visibility is not blocked by anything large, like a building or dense trees). Take turns signaling each other with the different objects. Which one works best?

2 Plan a meeting with the members of your spy network and devise a **code** using the flashes from your signal mirror. For example, one long repeating flash could mean, "It's safe to move forward," or a pattern of two

repeating short flashes could signal, "Stay back, danger ahead." Write down the meanings of the

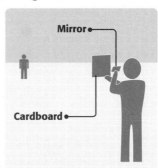

different signals and make sure everyone has a copy. When you're ready to send a coded signal, hold your mirror so you have a continuous ray of light aimed at your signal target. Then hold a piece of cardboard (or a similar object) in front of the mirror to block the light. By revealing and blocking the light repeatedly, you can create pattern of flashes.

A word to wise spies

● Do not use your signal mirror on or near a street, where drivers or bicyclists might be distracted by it.

WHAT'S THE SECRET?

In an age of amazing communications technology, the signal mirror is *still* considered one the best communication devices by search-and-rescue teams. Why? It doesn't need batteries or a charger, it doesn't take much skill to operate, and it's light, inexpensive, and easy to transport. And, most important, a flash from a signal mirror can be detected from more than *ten* miles away! Plus, for your escape and **evasion** purposes, the signal mirror has the added benefit of being a *silent* way to communicate.

Whether by night or day, the idea is *not* to maintain a steady beam of light. Instead, use the signal mirror to send out a series of flashes that can be noticed as a signal. Although any shiny object can be used for signaling, your signal mirror is designed to be easy to aim, and its flashes are highly visible. Even though the ideal time to use the signal mirror is on a clear day when the sun is high, your signal mirror will even work on a cloudy day.

SPYtales

You can send someone a signal with a flash of light, or even just by flashing a shopping bag! Oleg Gordievsky was the highest officer of the KGB (the intelligence service of the former Soviet Union) ever to work for British intelligence. For eleven years, he gave the British important Soviet secrets, including the names of **moles** who were working for the Soviets. But when Gordievsky himself was exposed by a mole inside the CIA named Aldrich Ames, the KGB began to watch him carefully. In 1985, Gordievsky knew that he needed to escape from Moscow (and **defect** to England) before he was arrested.

Gordievsky had a prearranged escape plan set up with his British contacts that was activated by a **danger signal**. What was the signal? Gordievsky stood on a certain Moscow street corner holding a shopping bag from Harrods (a famous British department store) at a particular time. A British intelligence officer drove by and spotted him...it was as simple as that!

Next, Gordievsky managed to escape his **surveillance** while he was out jogging, and he made his way to Leningrad. From there, Gordievsky moved on by bus and foot to a place called Viborg, on the border of the Soviet Union and Finland, and waited for his contacts to pick him up. Two British embassy employees arrived in a car, and

Gordievsky hid in the trunk, wrapped in a thermal blanket. Inside the trunk, Gordievsky waited as Soviet guards stopped the car. He could hear the guards talking to the driver as trained search dogs sniffed around the car for hidden goods and escaping defectors. He might have been caught had it not been for a trick of one of the British officials, who distracted the dogs by feeding them part of a sandwich! Gordievsky made it safely across the border into Finland and went on to England, where he later wrote an autobiography describing his KGB activities and his daring escape.

4

OPERATION Steer CLEAR

When you're in the middle of a getaway, it's *not* a good idea to stop and ask for directions. That's why you should never hit the road without your trusty compass! In fact, compasses are such helpful escape tools that spies and soldiers make sure they always have one handy, just in case they're captured.

But, of course, your compass can only guide you *if* you know how to use it properly. So give this operation a spin to make sure that your compass can help you out in a hurry.

● SOUTH   ● NORTH

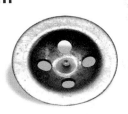

These fly buttons from a British military uniform could be converted into a compass. When the two buttons were stacked together, the top button could rotate freely. A dot on the edge of the button indicated which way was north. Two dots on the opposite side of the button marked south.

WHAT YOU DO
PART 1: FIND NORTH

The first step to mastering your compass is to learn how to find the direction north.

1 Take a look at the compass rose on this page and familiarize yourself with the four main directions: north, south, east, and west. In addition, the area between any two directions is known as the combination of the names (for example, the area between north and west is called "northwest").

2 Now look at your compass. As you can see, it has similar markings for north (N), south (S), east (E), and west (W). It also has a needle that will tell you which way is north. The black tip of the needle always points to the Earth's magnetic North Pole (pretty *cool*, huh?).

3 Hold your compass flat in your hand. Make sure the needle can rotate freely. Now, wait for the needle to stop jiggling. When it stops moving, the black tip of the needle will be pointing north.

4 Next, slowly rotate the compass in your hand. What do you notice? The needle moves a little bit, but always ends up pointing in the same direction (north).

5 Continue to rotate the compass until the black tip of the compass needle lines up with the north marking on the compass. Once they are lined up, you can clearly visualize where north is *and* you can easily figure out south, east, and west, too!

PART 2: GRIN AND BEARING

Now let your compass guide you around! In this part of the operation, you'll make your way to a **landmark** by using your compass to determine its **bearing** (or direction).

1 Stand outside in a park or an open area and look around you. Pick out a specific landmark that's at least 30 feet (9 m) away from you (such as a large tree) that you will walk toward after determining its bearing.

2 Face the tree and hold your compass out in front of you in one hand. As in Part 1, turn the compass until the black tip of the needle lines up with the north marking.

3 Now, look down at the compass housing and read the direction on your compass that's pointing toward the tree. This is the tree's bearing (for example, northeast).

4 Time for the game! While looking *only* at your compass, try to walk from where you are to the tree. The trick is to make sure that you stay "oriented" (in other words, keep your compass needle aligned with north so that you continue to head in a northeast direction). If the compass needle starts to move away from the north marking, adjust your path accordingly. You need to make sure the compass needle always stays on north.

5 Ask a friend to watch you to make sure you don't smack into anything while you're looking down (like the tree, if you're on the right track!). Are you able to get to the tree? How close are you?

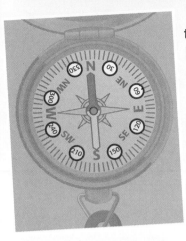

1 What if you wanted to head toward a landmark that was not exactly north, south, east, west, northwest, southwest, northeast, or southeast? Well, take a closer look at your compass, and you'll find black line markings for the 360 degrees of a circle.

Something that is north of you has a bearing of 0 degrees; something that's east of you has a bearing of 90 degrees; something that's south of you has a bearing of 180 degrees, and something that's west of you has a bearing of 270 degrees. A bearing can be *any* number from 0 to 360, allowing for very specific directions. Degrees are usually shown with the symbol (°).

2 How would you get back to the point that you started from in Part 2 of this operation? Ever heard of the expression "do a 180"? Well, that expression refers to the degree markings on your compass. Since half of a circle is 180 degrees, if you want to turn and face the opposite direction, you would turn 180 degrees.

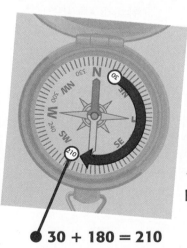

To "do a 180" and get back to where you started, you simply need to do some basic math. If you traveled at a bearing of 30 degrees to get to the tree, your "back bearing" would be 30 degrees plus

30 + 180 = 210

180 degrees (210 degrees). However, if the number of degrees you started out with was *higher* than 180, you would need to *subtract* 180 to get what is known as your "back bearing." Try it out and see if you find your way back to your starting point.

WHAT'S THE SECRET?

Your compass is made up of a magnetized steel needle rotating inside a case. It is able to direct you because of the natural magnetic force of the Earth, which pulls the needle toward the North Pole.

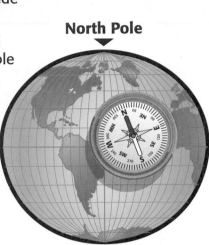

North Pole

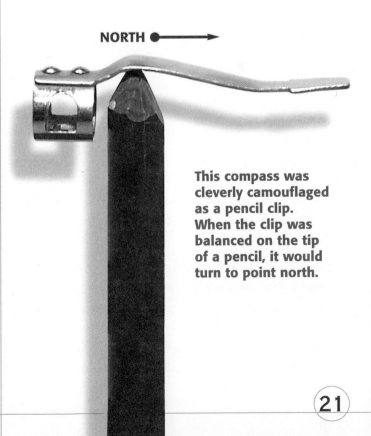

NORTH ●───→

This compass was cleverly camouflaged as a pencil clip. When the clip was balanced on the tip of a pencil, it would turn to point north.

#5 TRAIL Blazer

By now you should be feeling a bit more comfortable using your compass to help you get from one point to another. But don't stop there! Your compass can be a very nifty little gizmo to have around even when you *aren't* escaping. In fact, the more you handle your compass, the more uses you'll think up for it during your day-to-day spy operations. With all that practice, you'll be that much more prepared to use it for an actual escape. So, try this operation to learn how to use your compass to lead a friend to a hidden treasure!

STUFF YOU'LL NEED

- ◉◉ Compass
- Pencil and paper
- Small wooden stake (or stick)

YOUR NETWORK

- A friend to follow your trail

WHAT YOU DO

You're going to create a path for a friend to follow using your compass, leading to a hidden stake in the ground. The stake represents a spy's **dead drop** (a hiding place where the spy has left behind some materials for his **handler** to pick up).

Note: Instead of a stake, you can use any small object that can hide in the grass (like a coin).

1 First, find a large, open, grassy area, and stand in a specific spot, like in front of a certain tree or bench.

2 Find the direction north with your compass by aligning the needle and the north marking. Next, decide on the compass **bearing** that will take you in the direction you want to travel (for example, west). Turn back to **Operation Steer Clear** on page 19 if you need a review of how to do this.

3 Write down the bearing and the number of steps that you want to take in that direction (for example, west: 10 steps).

4 Looking carefully at your compass, take the number of steps in the direction you chose. Be sure to make your steps even. From the new point, choose another compass bearing (like northeast) and record the number of steps you want to take in that direction (for example, northeast: 15 steps).

5 steps northwest

15 steps northeast

10 steps west

Instructions:

West: 10 steps

Northeast: 15 steps

Northwest: 5 steps

5 Walk to your new spot, and from there, choose a third direction and number of steps and record them (for example, northwest: 5 steps).

6 Take the final number of steps in the correct direction. When you stop, press a small wooden stake into the ground where you're standing so that it's deep in the grass and can't be easily seen from far away.

7 Now test the skills of a friend! Have your friend try to find the stake by using your compass and following the directions you've recorded. Can she do it?

8 Have your friend write out a different set of directions for you to follow to find the stake, and see if *you* can do it!

The cache is in the tree house!

How about arranging a compass "treasure hunt" for several of your friends? Give each friend a set of compass directions that lead to a clue (you'll have to hide each person's clue in a different spot). The clue will tell your friend where to find a **cache** of spy gear that you've hidden somewhere. See who can get to the cache first!

WHAT'S THE SECRET?

Compasses help escaping spies in a number of ways. They can help spies reach a safe spot to hide, get them to a predetermined pick-up point, or even guide them into friendly territory. Pretty impressive for such a simple little instrument! But that's not all—in *addition* to helping spies get from one point to another, a compass can also enable a spy to locate a dead drop (as you learned in this operation) or even a cache of supplies hidden deep in a forest.

As you've seen, finding something hidden in a field can be tricky, even more so if it's buried underground. That's why spies sometimes use underground caches to stash things that they or another member of their **spy network** will need to get their hands on later.

During the Cold War (1945–1991), the KGB (the intelligence service of the former Soviet Union) filled a series of secret caches in different cities around the world. Inside the caches were arms, radio equipment, and even money that could be used by KGB agents for missions against their enemies in the event of an actual war or another crisis.

The KGB caches were scattered around North America, Europe, Israel, Turkey, Japan, and other parts of the world. Soviet handlers provided their agents with very specific directions to

the locations of the caches. The directions included detailed descriptions of **landmarks**, and told agents exactly how many steps to take in what direction to reach the cache. They also included instructions on how to open the caches, since some of them were booby-trapped with explosives that would destroy their contents if they were opened incorrectly.

Today, many years after the end of the conflict that led to their creation, it is believed that many of these abandoned caches still exist around the world (but they're highly dangerous...so don't start digging!).

SPYquest

(*continued from page 29*)

You hide behind a bush and watch as Justin searches. Finally, he gives up and leaves. You wait a few more minutes and then come out from your hiding place and go to the dead drop. You reach under the bush and pull out a fake rock with a hollow center. Inside is the secret message you've been

waiting for. You look around and don't see anyone nearby, so you start to relax a little. You pull out the message, unroll it, and give it a quick glance. Hmm... it's written in code. It'll only take you a minute to decode it, so you pull out your pencil and start working.

Flash!

You quickly turn around, and there's Justin with a camera pointed at you! Yikes! You were so absorbed in your message that you didn't hear him creeping up behind you.

"Hey! What do you think you're doing?" you ask him angrily.

"I got some tips that you were involved in spy activities, and now I have some evidence!" Justin replies smugly.

"Spy activities?" you ask, trying to sound natural. "I have no idea what you're talking about. I just came to find some class notes that I dropped here by accident on my way to school this morning."

"Nice try!" he sneers. "Notes inside a fake rock? And who takes notes in *code*?" he asks, eyeing the message. "This is going to make a great cover story!"

You should've been more careful with a nosy reporter on the prowl!

■ This was a dead end. Turn back and try again!

Star SEARCH

#6

Your compass is a great tool to help you find your way during an escape. But what if you don't have one handy? What now? You could wish upon a lucky star and hope you find your way. Or, you could *use* a lucky star to help guide you! Try this operation to find out how to use the North Star to navigate your way to safety.

WHAT YOU DO

Note: This operation needs to take place outside on a clear night.

1 Since you'll be using your compass at night, you'll need to get it ready to glow in the dark. So, before you go outside, open the compass and hold its face up to a light. This will make the compass glow brightly enough to be read in the dark.

2 Go outside on a clear night and stand in an area where you have a good view of the sky. Make sure a senior spy joins you. You can use your spy light ring to light your way.

3 To find the North Star for the first time, you'll use your compass, but later you'll learn how to locate it on your own. Place your compass flat on your hand, allowing the needle to move freely. When the needle has stopped, the black tip will be pointing north.

4 Look up into the sky in the direction north.

5 Try to make out a bright array of seven stars (a constellation) known as the Big Dipper. The stars are grouped together so that they seem to form a ladle. Three stars make what looks like a curved handle, and four stars form the ladle's bowl or "dipper." Depending on the time of year, the Big Dipper can be upside down, or on its side, but it will always be in the northern sky, and it will always guide you to the North Star.

Big Dipper

Harriet Tubman

The Big Dipper was called the Drinking Gourd by slaves in the American South before the Civil War (1861–1865). They used the Drinking Gourd to locate the North Star, which guided them to freedom during their dangerous escapes from slavery.

The Underground Railroad was the secret **code** name given to an escape route used by slaves to get to the North, where slavery was outlawed. Escaping slaves (known as "passengers") were led by "conductors" using covered wagons or carts that had false bottoms to hide slaves. The slaves were taken from one "station" (the home of a supporter of the Underground Railroad) to another on their journey to freedom.

Harriet Tubman was the most famous conductor of the Underground Railroad. After escaping to the North alone by following the North Star, she risked her life to return to the South nineteen times and lead more than three hundred slaves to safety. During the Civil War, Harriet Tubman continued to use her courage for the cause of freedom. She served as a nurse, a scout, and even a *spy* for the Northern army.

6 Imagine a line connecting the two stars at the front of the "dipper" (which are called the "guides"), and then imagine the line extending farther, in the direction that the ladle's bowl is facing. Follow the imaginary line with your eyes. When your eyes have followed the line a distance that's five times longer than the distance between the two guides, you should be looking at the North Star, which is known by astronomers as Polaris.

7 After finding the North Star, imagine a line drawn from the star to the Earth. Where the line hits the horizon is the general direction north. Find a **landmark** at that point and use it as a guide.

8 Practice locating the North Star over several nights until you're good enough at spotting it *without* using your compass first.

MORE FROM HEADQUARTERS

1 If you have trouble finding the North Star by using the Big Dipper alone, it might help to find another constellation, Cassiopeia (pronounced "Kass-ee-uhp-ee-uh"). This constellation looks like a "W" on its side, and it's on the opposite side of Polaris from the Big Dipper. In Cassiopeia, the center of the "W" points to Polaris.

2 If you live in the Southern Hemisphere (or happen to be there on a spy mission), you won't be able to use the North Star to guide you (since it's only visible in the *Northern* Hemisphere!). Instead, you can use the Southern Cross. To find the Southern Cross, use your compass to find south. Then look into the southern sky to find four stars that form a small cross known as the Southern Cross. It's small, but easy to recognize. The two guiding stars form the long axis (or line) of the cross.

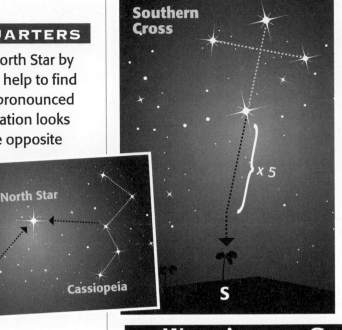

Imagine a distance five times longer than the distance between the two guiding stars. At the end of the line is the general direction of south.

WHAT'S THE SECRET?

Polaris is called the North Star because it is located almost directly above the North Pole all year-round. For centuries, people around the world have used the North Star and other constellations (like the Southern Cross) to navigate at sea and when traveling over land. However, since the North Star is actually not a very bright star, it helps to use other constellations like the Big Dipper to locate it.

SPYquest

(continued from page 9)

You decide to follow Justin since you'd really like to find out what he could possibly know, and what he's trying to discover. You wait until he passes your hiding place, and then slip out from behind the tree and start to tail him. You make sure he doesn't notice you by moving so silently that he doesn't hear you.

Justin goes back to school and enters a classroom with a bunch of kids, closing the door behind him.

You notice a sign on the door that says this is the weekly meeting of the newspaper club. You sure would like to know what Justin is reporting. The only problem is, you can't hear much from where you are.

You have to decide what to do. You could put your ear against the door and listen in on the meeting, or you could wait until the end of the meeting and then search the room for clues. You could also

call an emergency meeting of your spy network to see if anyone knows what's going on.

- If you decide to try to listen in on the meeting, turn to **page 33**.

- If you decide to search the room for clues, turn to **page 41**.

- If you decide to meet with your spy network to see if they know anything about the newspaper's plans, turn to **page 12**.

Bug OUT

7

No spy is safe without a **bug-out kit** (and we're *not* talking about a product for getting rid of roaches!). In the spy world, a bug-out kit is an escape kit, filled with essential items that spies have ready in case they need to quickly "bug out" (or *get out*) of an area. The kit contains the escape aids and survival items spies need to make their getaways and avoid capture. Want to ensure that you have a better chance of escaping when you have to bug out of town? Then start packing!

WHAT YOU DO

1 Think about the types of things that you would most want and need to have with you during an escape. The goal is to pack as little as possible and to include only the most useful items so your kit isn't bulky or so heavy that it slows you down.

2 Write down ten items that you choose from the list below to include in your kit. Although you may *want* to take more than ten items, you'll have to limit your choices!

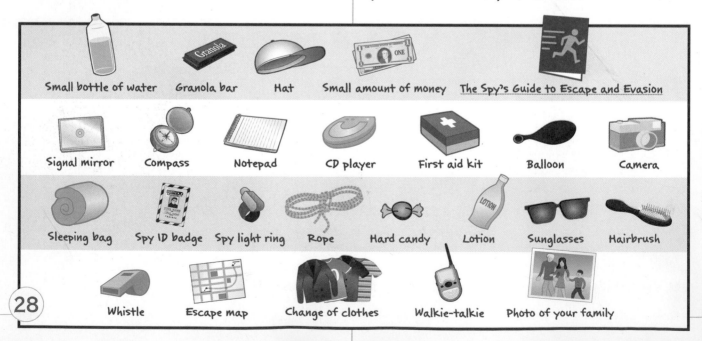

Small bottle of water   Granola bar   Hat   Small amount of money   The Spy's Guide to Escape and Evasion

Signal mirror   Compass   Notepad   CD player   First aid kit   Balloon   Camera

Sleeping bag   Spy ID badge   Spy light ring   Rope   Hard candy   Lotion   Sunglasses   Hairbrush

Whistle   Escape map   Change of clothes   Walkie-talkie   Photo of your family

3 Do you think like an expert escapee? Rate your choices according to the table in the **What's the Secret** section of this operation (on page 30). Then, modify your list as needed.

4 Next, collect the items on your list. Place all of your emergency items in your fanny pack. If you don't have a fanny pack, you can use another type of container, like a small tote bag or an old backpack. Whatever you decide to use, make sure that it isn't big and bulky, and that it doesn't look out of place (you might look strange carting a shoebox around with you outside!). Store your completed bug-out kit in a safe place at headquarters where it would be easy to grab in a hurry.

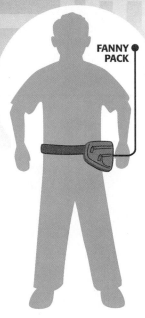

FANNY PACK

WHAT'S THE SECRET?

A well-planned bug-out kit can increase your chances of getting to safety during an escape, since you'll have all the essential survival items you need. An important thing to remember is that preparing your bug-out kit is not the same as planning for a long trip! You should only include the items that would be immediately useful as you hide from enemies, wait to be picked up, or complete a short journey to a safe place.

How did you do selecting items for your bug-out kit? Did you think more like a true escapee or someone packing for a vacation? Turn the page, and you'll see we've assigned points to each item based on its usefulness. Add up your total number of points to see how you did!

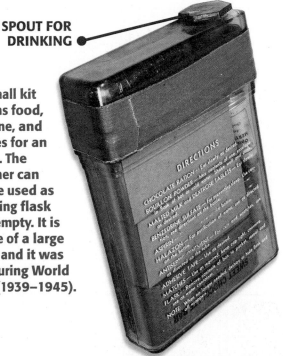

SPOUT FOR DRINKING

This small kit contains food, medicine, and supplies for an escape. The container can even be used as a drinking flask when empty. It is the size of a large wallet, and it was used during World War II (1939–1945).

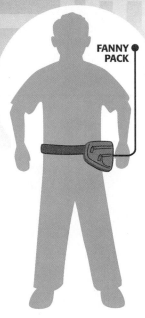

SPYquest

(continued from page 9)

As you approach the dead drop the next day after school, you see Justin poking around in the bushes nearby. This can't be a coincidence!

You're pretty sure that Justin won't be able to find your dead drop, but having him so close to it makes you nervous. You want to wait for him to leave so you can get your hands safely on the secret message. At the same time, you think it might be a good idea to leave right now and call an emergency meeting with the members of your spy network, Spy Force One, to see if they know anything about what's going on.

■ If you decide to wait until Justin leaves and then unload the drop before he can find it, turn to **page 24**.

■ If you decide to meet with Spy Force One, turn to **page 12**.

Item	Points	Reason
Bottle of water	1	It's a good habit to drink water all day, but it's also an essential survival item.
Granola bar	1	Not just a snack, it could be breakfast, lunch, *and* dinner for an escapee!
Hat	1	Keeps the sun out of your eyes and your head warm and dry.
Small amount of money	1	Comes in handy for making phone calls, paying bus fare, or buying food.
This book	-1	Leave it at headquarters! You've studied the contents, anyway…right?
Signal mirror	1	Useful for flashing your friends for help.
Compass	1	*Where* would you be without it?
Notepad	0	Not essential!
CD player	0	Know how to hum a tune?
First aid kit	1	Hope you don't need it, but it's best to be prepared.
Balloon	1	See page 31.
Camera	0	You should focus on getting *away*, not on taking snapshots.
Sleeping bag	0	Too big!
Spy ID badge	-1	Are you kidding? Hide it at headquarters.
Spy light ring	1	Helps you find your way after dark.
Rope	1	Can be useful to help you climb, tie things together, or pull something along.
Hard candy	1	Mmmm…gives you a quick energy boost!
Lotion	0	You can live without it.
Sunglasses	0	Might look cool, but a hat serves the same purpose.
Hairbrush	0	You're escaping, not going to a party!
Whistle	1	Can be heard from far away and takes less energy than yelling for help.
Escape map	1	But of course!
Change of clothes	0	Remember, this isn't a vacation!
Walkie-talkie	0	Can only transmit over a short distance and is too bulky, anyway.
Photo of your family	-1	A sweet idea, but *not* a good one! It could blow your spy **cover**!

1 point
This item is either an essential part of your bug-out kit or something that would be useful to have.

0 points
This item might be nice to have with you if you could take more than ten items, but you can't, so leave it at home!

-1 point
Oh, no! This item is something you *really* shouldn't have with you (especially if you get caught!). Subtract a point for choosing this item!

If you scored between 8 and 10, awesome job! You've got great survival instincts. If you scored between 5 and 7, you're on the right track and have a good idea of the things you need most during an escape. If you scored between 0 and 4, we hope you don't plan to bug out anytime soon! Go back and reevaluate the items you chose. Remember, your kit is only meant to contain a *few* of the most important emergency items that you would need for a short period of time.

Surprised to find the balloon on the list of useful items? Well, believe it or not, a balloon can actually serve many purposes in the great outdoors. It can be an emergency water

How'd you do?

Score	Rank
8–10 points	Escape Expert!
5–7 points	Strong Survivor
0–4 points	Bug-Out Beginner

bottle, a trail marker, and even a pillow! And it demonstrates why the *most* important thing to have with you at all times is your imagination! In a fix, you can improvise and use whatever you have with you to survive.

MORE FROM HEADQUARTERS

Just like you created an escape plan with your family in case of an emergency (in **Operation Great Escape**), it's a good idea to have a home emergency kit to help you out in the event of any type of disaster (including a power outage—something that isn't too rare!). Work together with your family to develop the kit, and be sure to include essentials such as nonperishable food, water, a flashlight (check those batteries!), matches (for adult use only!), and candles.

SPYquest

(*continued from page 37*)

You decide that the story about Ms. Lightly is a better idea. The next day at school, you look for Justin and agree to give him some information to get him off your back. You find him in the hall after class and take him aside. You tell him that you're tired of him following you around and that you're ready to give him an interview.

"Well, okay," he says suspiciously. "I've been watching you and your friends, and the stuff you're up to makes

me think that you're spies! Plus, I got an anonymous tip that there was a spy network operating at school. Can you explain that to me?"

You make up a story about how you and your friends are working on a secret school project with Ms. Lightly. It has nothing to do with spies or spying, you assure him. By the time you're through telling your story, you're pretty sure Justin is convinced.

But you should have known that all good reporters check their facts!

Justin asks Ms. Lightly about the secret project and she acts surprised, saying that she doesn't know anything about it and has never asked you to do anything of the sort. Now Justin is even *more* suspicious of you than before...and so is Ms. Lightly! It's going to be even harder to avoid Justin and his snooping.

■ This was a dead end. Turn back and try again!

OPERATION ROLL With It

Spies have come up with lots of creative ways to hide their escape supplies. Escape maps can be hidden inside pens, hairbrushes, and even in decks of playing cards! Maps have been printed on handkerchiefs with invisible ink, and they've been drawn on silk fabric or special rice paper that doesn't rustle when you unfold it. Are you as crafty as the people who came up with those ideas? Well, start by disguising a map for yourself, and you'll get there soon enough!

STUFF YOU'LL NEED

- **Thin white tissue paper (like the kind you find inside a gift box)**
- **Scissors**
- **Ruler**
- **Pencil**
- **Ballpoint pen (the kind that can be unscrewed)**

WHAT YOU DO

1 Cut out a small square of tissue paper to create your map (no larger than 3 inches, or 7.5 cm). If you're using tissue from a gift box, make sure that it's white, and not too rumpled or torn.

2 Copy your escape map from **Operation Great Escape** onto the tissue paper. Use the pencil to make your drawing as detailed as possible, but most important, label the major **landmarks** and make it clear enough to read and follow.

3 Unscrew the pen barrel and remove the ink tube.

4 Fold your tissue paper map in half and then tightly roll it around the ink tube so that it's small enough to fit back inside the pen.

5 Put the pen back together again. The pen should still work with the map inside.

6 Keep the pen with you at all times and be prepared for an escape!

❶ TOP OF PEN BARREL

❷ INK TUBE

❸ BOTTOM OF PEN BARREL

MORE FROM HEADQUARTERS

Can you think of other things you can hide in the barrel of a pen? How about wrapping a secret message around the ink tube? To pass the message, just loan the pen to your friend! To be extra secure, put the message in **code**.

WHAT'S THE SECRET?

In the spy world, an ordinary object that is modified to hide something is known as a **concealment**. The idea is to fool others into thinking they're looking at a normal, everyday item. Spies and prisoners of war have used a variety of concealments to aid in their escapes. Sometimes the concealments were smuggled to them in prison. Other times, the concealed escape aids were hidden on the prisoners' bodies all along (like inside a false tooth!), unknown to their captors. One clever concealment used during World War II (1939–1945) was an ordinary-looking hairbrush that opened up to reveal an entire escape kit, complete with a tissue paper map, a compass, and a miniature saw.

COMPASS

This silk escape map was hidden inside a fountain pen, which also concealed a compass. It was used during World War II.

SPYquest

(continued from page 27)

You tiptoe over to the door, press your ear against it, and try to listen in on the meeting. You can make out a few words like "cover" and "dead." Are they talking about spies or just general newspaper issues? You lean in a little closer against the door when all of a sudden, you realize that it wasn't closed all the way. *Crash!* You lose your balance and fall into the room. Everyone stares at you, and Justin runs over and points an accusing finger at you.

"Look everyone!" he shouts. "Here's some spying going on right under our noses! It must be true that there's a spy network operating right here at school, and we get to break the story!"

It's going to be hard to convince Justin that you weren't spying since you've been caught red-handed!

■ This was a dead end. Turn back and try again!

OPERATION Stealthy SPY

In some of the most daring and dangerous prison escapes of all time, prisoners of war slipped out of heavily guarded areas without ever being seen or heard. How did they do it? By knowing all the obstacles in their way, by timing their moves just right, and by relying on their abilities to hide and move silently. Do you have what it takes to *get out of jail free*? Test your escaping abilities with a noisy obstacle course and see!

STUFF YOU'LL NEED

- **Noisy materials (like dry leaves, newspaper, empty cans with rocks inside, bubble wrap, and so on)**
- **Blindfold**
- **Flashlight**
- **Spy light ring**

YOUR NETWORK

- **A friend to play the role of the guard**
- **A senior spy to supervise**

WHAT YOU DO

1 First, find a large outdoor space where you can set up your noisy obstacle course. You'll be doing this at night, so make sure to find a location that's safe (like a backyard).

2 Next, create an obstacle course full of materials that rustle, creak, crinkle, and clank. The course should include things like dry leaves, empty cans (place stones inside them for more noise!), newspapers, cellophane paper, and bubble wrap. Use your imagination to come up with different noisemakers.

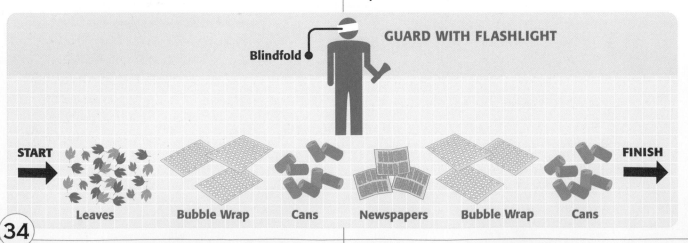

Blindfold — GUARD WITH FLASHLIGHT

START → Leaves — Bubble Wrap — Cans — Newspapers — Bubble Wrap — Cans → FINISH

3 Once it's dark outside, you can test how well you can move through the obstacle course without getting caught. One friend will be the "guard." He should put on the blindfold (so he can't use his night vision) and hold the flashlight. He should then stand in one place about ten steps away from the obstacle course.

4 When you're ready, start to move slowly and quietly through the course, using your spy light ring to help you avoid the noisemakers. If the guard hears your steps, he should yell "Freeze!" and point the flashlight in the direction of the noise. If you're caught in the light beam, then you're captured, and you become the guard. If you're not caught in the light beam, you can continue moving. The senior spy should help determine whether or not you've been caught (since the guard can't see for himself). See if you can make it all the way through the course without alerting the guard!

Here are some tips for moving without being heard:

- Make your steps and movements extremely slow. Running though a pile of leaves, for example, makes a lot more noise than someone taking very careful steps.

- Try to time your movements so that they go along with noises in the environment. For example, take steps when you hear cars going by or a plane flying overhead. These other noises might mask any sounds you make.

MORE FROM HEADQUARTERS

Try this activity again, but this time, invite more friends to join you. Decide on a certain amount of time you will have for the entire group to move through the obstacle course. See how many friends can escape to safety in time!

WHAT'S THE SECRET?

In this operation, you worked on moving without being *heard*, but in a real escape situation, you'd also have to move without being *seen*.

A guard (or anyone who's watching) will most often detect your presence by your movement, color, and shape. For this reason, being still or moving slowly (and wearing **camouflage** clothing) can give you the best odds of not getting caught during an escape. And of course, being as quiet as possible will always improve your chances of sneaking away from your enemy undetected.

You can observe this rule in nature when animals are trying to escape from predators. Some animals, like rabbits or deer, freeze when they think they're in danger since any movement would give them away. Freezing is as close as they can get to being invisible! Or, you can think like an ostrich—these birds fall to the ground and lie still so that predators mistake them for bushes and don't attack. Later they sneak away (pretty sharp thinking for a birdbrain, huh?).

OPERATION DECOY DECOY Play

DECOY

Another important escape technique involves outsmarting **counterspies** with a **decoy**. Using a decoy, you can fool counterspies into thinking they're watching *you*, while they're actually watching someone (or something) who just *looks* like you! Ready to dupe some counterspies? Then try this operation and see how a clever decoy can be an escaping spy's *best friend*!

STUFF YOU'LL NEED

- **Sunglasses**
- **Hat**
- **Jacket**
- **Watch**

YOUR NETWORK

- **A friend to serve as a decoy**
- **A friend to serve as the counterspy**

WHAT YOU DO

1 Challenge a friend to a game of **surveillance** tag, in which you're the spy, and she's the counterspy. The counterspy wins if she can maintain surveillance on you for an hour, and you win if you can lose her before then.

2 One way of shaking off surveillance is to make the counterspy think she's watching you, when she really isn't! To do this, you're going to use a decoy, in this case a body double (just like they use in Hollywood!).

3 Before the game, put on a pair of sunglasses, a hat, and a jacket.

4 Next, arrange to meet your body double during the hour of the game. This friend should be roughly the same height and weight as you are. Plan to meet at your friend's house.

5 Start timing, and move around your neighborhood as normal. When you're sure that the counterspy is watching you, head to your friend's house and go inside.

6 Once you're inside and away from any windows, make sure your friend is wearing similar pants to yours. Then, give your friend the jacket, hat, and sunglasses you're wearing so that your "double" will look a lot like you. If your friend has any features that are very different from yours (like hair color, for example), make sure the clothing hides them.

7 Next, have your friend suddenly dash out of the house and run away from the counterspy. The counterspy will run after your body double if she bought the decoy and thought it was you.

8 Now you can sit back and relax while you wait for the counterspy to figure out what happened, because you've won the game!

MORE FROM HEADQUARTERS

Switch roles with the counterspy, and give your friend a chance to escape *your* surveillance. See what clever decoys she can come up with!

WHAT'S THE SECRET?

In this operation, you created an illusion that would make a magician proud. Just like a magician, you distracted the counterspy by making her watch the wrong thing. That gave you time to pull off your magic trick, which, in this case, was to *disappear*!

Decoys have been used in many of the great escapes in history, including the escape from Colditz Castle that you'll read about on page 38. A simple decoy isn't intended to fool someone forever, but just long enough to help the escapee get ahead of his pursuers.

(continued from page 12)

You decide to use a decoy. The next morning, you look out your window and see Justin waiting for you outside your house again. You call up Sam and ask him to come over, but you tell him to enter secretly through the backyard.

Since you and Sam are the same height, you hope that by putting on your jacket and hat, he'll pass for you from a distance. After checking to make sure that Justin is still outside, you send Sam, dressed like you, running out the front door past Justin. You watch from the window as Justin takes off after Sam. You can see Justin's camera dangling around

his neck. He's up to no good! But at least now you've bought yourself some time to get your secret message from the dead drop and to think up a plan for how to deal with Justin next time he comes around.

You realize that Justin isn't going to leave you alone until he *thinks* that he has his story. Maybe it would be best to agree to talk to him, and tell him a cover story so he'll leave you alone and let you get back to your spy operations.

Now you just need to come up with some kind of story about why you've

been secretive. Hmmm. How about telling him that you're working on a secret school project for Ms. Lightly? That might just sound official and important enough for him. Or you could say that you're working on a science-fair project that you want to keep secret because you don't want anyone to steal your idea.

- If you decide to tell Justin that you're working on a secret school project for Ms. Lightly, turn to **page 31**.

- If you decide to tell him that you're working on a science-fair project, turn to **page 43**.

ESCAPE FROM COLDITZ CASTLE!

Decoys were the key to a daring escape from Colditz Castle, a fortress used by the Germans as a high-security prison camp during World War II (1939–1945). Many of the prisoners sent to Colditz were considered "flight risks" because they had attempted to escape earlier. But what the Germans didn't realize was that by putting all of these determined minds together, they were creating what became known as the Colditz Escape Academy!

The Germans were under the impression that Colditz was "escape proof" because of its drastic security measures (including hundreds of prison guards, a parade held four times each day to count prisoners, guard dogs, machine-gun posts, and searchlights!). However, there were more than *300* escape attempts made by Colditz prisoners during the war. Even though the majority of the attempts failed, 130 men managed to escape from Colditz, and 32 of them made it safely back to their homes (the rest, unfortunately, were either recaptured or killed).

One successful escape plan started with the discovery of a loose bolt on a manhole in a park near the castle, where the prisoners were taken for exercise. In the park, a group of Dutch prisoners gathered around the manhole while two escapees climbed inside, unseen by the guards. A piece of glass that was painted black and looked like a bolt was replaced instead of the loose bolt, so that guards would think the manhole was locked (and the escapees could literally "break out" after dark!).

To make sure the escaping prisoners wouldn't be missed during the next prison-wide parade, a group of inmates held up dummies to be counted instead of them.

An inmate who was a sculptor made the two dummy heads out of plaster, and painted them to be remarkably lifelike. The heads were then placed on long Dutch army coats and were topped off with caps. The dummy duo, nicknamed Max and Moritz, bought the two Dutch escapees enough time to successfully travel to Switzerland. They also allowed four more men to break out the same way and were used for several months for other escape attempts until prison guards finally discovered them and put an end to their careers.

Colditz Castle

OPERATION
ROCKET
Science

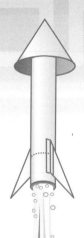

How can you make sure that a rescuer picks up your signal and comes to help you during your escape? Why not use something they'll be sure to notice, like, say…a rocket! Sound a little *out of this world*? Then, *launch* into this next activity and see how it works!

STUFF YOU'LL NEED

- **35 mm film canister (use one where the lid seals inside the canister—Fuji film uses these)**
- **Paper**
- **Scissors**
- **Ruler**
- **Tape**
- **Water**
- **Half of an Alka-Seltzer tablet (ask a senior spy to give you one)**

WHAT YOU DO

1 The first step is to build the base of your rocket. Cut a regular 8.5 x 11-inch (21.5 x 28-cm) piece of paper in half so that you have a 5.5 x 8.5-inch (14 x 21.5-cm) rectangle.

|← 8.5 inches →|

|← 5.5 inches →|

2 Place the paper on a table in front of you and put the film canister (without its lid) facing outward on a short edge of the paper.

CANISTER ●

3 Roll the paper around the film canister until the paper makes a tight tube around the canister. Then tape the other side of the paper to itself. This is the body of the rocket.

George Blake was a British intelligence officer who became a **mole** and spied for the Soviet Union during the 1950s. After he was caught, Blake made a daring escape from a British prison that involved a signaling device—but not a rocket. Blake was lucky enough to have a radio.

After his conviction, Blake was held at a prison in London called Wormwood Scrubs. But soon enough, he and his friend, Sean Bourke, who had recently been released from the prison, planned his escape.

On the evening of his escape, Blake waited until most of the guards and prisoners were at a film show in the prison theater. He then contacted Bourke on a radio that had been smuggled into prison, letting Bourke know that he was ready to break out. Blake knocked loose a bar in his cell window, slid onto a roof, and made his way to the ground. Bourke waited on the other side of the wall as Blake climbed up a rope ladder he had knit (with the help of some knitting needles!), and the two sped away in a getaway car. Blake was smuggled into East Germany by another friend, who hid him inside a blanket box in a van. He eventually made his way to the Soviet Union, where Bourke later joined him.

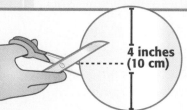

4 inches
(10 cm)

4 Now you're going to make the cone of your rocket. Cut a 4-inch (10-cm) circle out of paper. Cut a slit in the circle from one edge to the center of the circle.

5 Slide one side of the slit over the other to form a cone that will fit on top of the rocket. Keep sliding the edges to make the cone's opening only a bit larger than the opening of the paper tube.

6 When the cone is the right size, tape it along the slit to hold its shape. Then tape the cone to the end of the paper tube (opposite the film canister) so that it becomes the point of your rocket.

7 Make triangular fins for the base of your rocket and tape them in place.

CANISTER

8 Snap the lid onto the canister and test to see if the rocket will stand up on its end. If the rocket topples over, try adjusting the body of the rocket, the nose, or the fins to make sure that the weight is evenly distributed.

CAP

ALKA-SELTZER (HALF TABLET)

CANISTER (WITH WATER INSIDE)

9 Now it's time to go outside for a rocket launch. Remove the lid from the canister, turn the rocket upside down, and then fill the canister about ¼ full of water.

10 Drop half of an Alka-Seltzer tablet into the water, and then quickly snap the lid back on the canister. Turn the rocket right side up and set it down on the ground. Quickly stand back for blastoff!

MORE FROM HEADQUARTERS

1 Can you get your rocket to fly higher? Try launching it again using more or less water, and see if that makes a difference. How about using more or less of the Alka-Seltzer tablet?

2 Experiment with different rocket shapes and fin designs as well as different film canisters. What effects do these changes have on the rocket's flight?

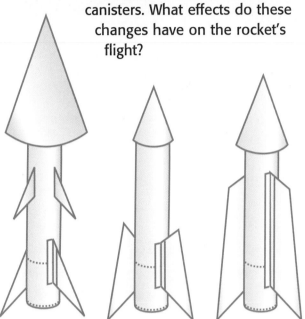

WHAT'S THE SECRET?

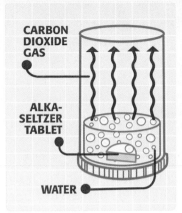

CARBON DIOXIDE GAS

ALKA-SELTZER TABLET

WATER

Your rocket flies because of a chemical reaction that takes place when Alka-Seltzer dissolves in water, forming carbon dioxide gas. When the gas first begins to form, it's easily contained in the canister. But as more gas forms, it begins to build up pressure inside the canister. Eventually, the pressure of the gas is greater than the force that holds the lid in place. The exploding gas pops the lid off, and the rocket takes off.

A word to wise spies

● Only launch your rocket *outside*.

(continued from page 27)

You wait and wait for the meeting to end, hidden behind the corner in the hallway. Finally, an hour later, you hear the door open, and you duck into another room as the kids leave. Then you enter the meeting room to look for clues that could give you an idea of what they're investigating. You scan the room from top to bottom. You see a desk drawer that's open slightly and has a bunch of papers sticking out of it. You start to look inside the drawer, hoping to find some notes from the newspaper club meeting, when you hear a voice behind you.

"What are you doing in here, and why are you looking through those papers?" asks a stern Mr. Shader. "You aren't part of the newspaper club, and you shouldn't be in here after hours. It's against school policy!"

You try to make up some kind of excuse, but Mr. Shader won't hear any of it. Well, at least Justin won't be able to follow you around after school for the next week, because you've got detention!

■ This was a dead end. Write, "I will not break the rules" a hundred times on the blackboard, and then turn back and try again.

#12 TAP Code

Imagine this: Two captured spies are sitting in separate rooms. They aren't using any electric devices (like pagers or cell phones), they aren't passing each other notes, and they're not saying a word. But *somehow* they're managing to communicate with each other to plan their escape. How? By *tapping* into a secret **code** that uses nothing but their knuckles and the wall between them. Want us to let you in on the secret? Ready, set, tap!

STUFF YOU'LL NEED

- **A wall**
- **Pencil and paper**

YOUR NETWORK

- **A friend to receive your messages**

WHAT YOU DO

1 Have a look at the grid below. There are five rows and five columns, and the letters of the alphabet are arranged inside.

	1	2	3	4	5
1	A	B	C	D	E
2	F	G	H	I	J
3	L	M	N	O	P
4	Q	R	S	T	U
5	V	W	X	Y	Z

Did you notice that the letter K is missing from the grid? That's because there are only twenty-five spaces in the grid, but there are twenty-six letters in the alphabet. So, whenever you have a message that includes the letter K, you'll have to use the letter C instead.

2 Now let's learn how to use the code. Say you wanted to tap the word "Hi."

3 Find "H" on the grid. Notice it's in the third column, second row (remember that columns go down and rows go across).

Tap!
Tap!
Tap!
(pause)
Tap!
Tap!

4 To tap an "H" on the wall, simply tap three times on the wall, wait a second, then tap two times.

5 The letter "I" is in the fourth column, second row. So you would tap four times, wait a second, and then tap two times.

6 Have you figured it out? All you do is tap out each letter, using the column number and then the row number.

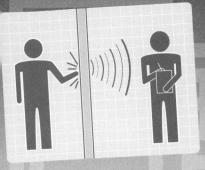

7 Practice the tap code by tapping your name to a friend on the other side of a wall and see if he can figure out your message. It will help, at first, if he writes down the number of taps as he hears them, then decodes the message after you're done tapping. Have your friend tap something back to you and see if you can get it!

MORE FROM HEADQUARTERS

1 Some walls can be pretty thick, and it would be hard to hear sounds through them. Try using two cups to amplify the sounds. Get as close as you can to your friend on the other side of the wall. Each of you put the open end of the cup on the wall, press your ear against the cup bottom, and tap the wall. Can you hear the tap code any better using this method?

 2 Test your tap code skills on the Spy U web site (**www.scholastic.com/spy**)!

SPYtales

The tap code was developed during World War II (1939–1945) and was used often by American prisoners of war during the Vietnam War (1964–1975). The prisoners became so good at the code that they could communicate with ease. They made sure to keep from being caught tapping by watching shadows and using water puddles as mirrors. The prisoners would often sign off by tapping the following code: "GNST"—"Good night, sleep tight."

WHAT'S THE SECRET?

The tap code is an effective way to communicate with someone on the other side of a wall. To make communication even easier, try to use abbreviations to cut down on the number of letters you have to tap.

(continued from page 37)

The next day after school, you wait for Justin to start following you, and then you turn around and approach him. You tell him that you don't like the fact that he's been following you around, but you're ready to give him an interview if he'll leave you alone. He agrees to leave you alone if you give him what he needs. Then he fires a bunch of questions at you.

"Are you working as a spy? Are you involved in secret activities? Who's working with you?"

You already thought your answers through carefully during lunch and are prepared to answer him.

Of course you're not a spy, you tell him. You've just been busy working on your science-fair project, which you're trying to keep secret so that no one steals your idea. You explain to him that your project is the reason you've been searching in the bushes, and you even make up something about collecting soil samples and testing for acid rain. Then you tell him that your spy network friends are actually part of a science club.

"It's really very interesting. Why don't you come with me next time I test the soil?" you offer generously.

"Uh, that's okay, I've got to work on another lead story," he mumbles as he turns to walk away. "Sorry for bothering you."

Well, it looks like you've done a good job putting Justin's curiosity to rest! Your spy identity and network will remain safe for now. Good job *escaping* unwanted attention!

■ Congratulations! Quest accomplished!

Yes!

During World War II (1939–1945), packages called "naughty parcels" were sent to British prisoners of war. They contained concealed escape devices to help the prisoners make their getaways.

Naughty PARCEL

Clayton Hutton, a British intelligence officer who cleverly concealed escape devices during World War II.

A saw hidden inside bootlaces? A compass stashed inside a walnut? What kind of mind does it take to invent such ingenious hiding places? Someone like British gadget mastermind Clayton "Clutty" Hutton, the brain behind some of the extraordinary escape devices and **concealments** you've already read about in this guide, plus a whole lot more.

Hutton was fascinated by the world of "escapology." He was known not to do things by the book, and was even called eccentric (a polite word for "weird!") by his bosses. But those qualities made him the perfect person to do an important job at a special branch of British intelligence known as MI9 (Military Intelligence 9). During World War II, MI9 was in charge of finding ways to help captured soldiers and downed pilots get safely home. In other words, it was all about escape and **evasion**!

Hutton's mission at MI9 was to make escape aids that were disguised well enough to be carried by soldiers and not be seized during enemy searches. He began by reading stories of true escapes from World War I (1914–1918), and soon decided that everyone flying over enemy territory should be issued a map and compass in case their aircraft was shot down.

These cuff links had compasses hidden inside them.

First, Hutton designed a variety of tiny compasses that could be hidden inside pens, buttons, cuff links, or collar studs. The compasses could be carried, hidden in belts, and sewn into uniforms. More than two million compasses of Hutton's design were made during the war years and issued to those who took part in flying operations.

Next, Hutton tackled maps. He had maps transferred onto pieces of white silk so they could pass as handkerchiefs and wouldn't rustle when unfolded. Every pilot was issued a map of the country he flew over as part of his flying kit. Hutton also discovered a Japanese variety of thin, non-rustling rice paper, perfect for escape

These escape maps were made of fabric so they wouldn't rustle when opened.

maps. These maps were concealed in pens and pipes, slipped inside book covers, and even hidden inside the thinnest music records.

But Hutton didn't stop with maps and compasses! He designed a tiny hacksaw that could be hidden in the sole of a shoe to help prisoners cut their way out during an escape. He had surgical saws (thin pieces of jagged wire designed for brain surgeons) hidden inside bootlaces. And he crafted an escape boot, which was a fleece-lined flying boot that could be cut off with a small knife hidden at the top. In mere minutes, a soldier could transform his boots into ordinary black walking shoes and use the inside of the fleece-lined upper boot to assemble a vest. And just like that, he could be transformed from an escaping soldier to an ordinary peasant whom no one would bother!

One of the items Hutton was most famous for was an "escape box," which was a cigarette box filled with escape supplies. The box included enough emergency food to survive 48 hours (nothing fancy—just malted milk tablets and hard candies), water-purifying

This military boot could be converted into a regular shoe by cutting off the top part.

tablets, matches, energy tablets, a bottle, a razor with a magnetized blade (to make a compass), soap, a needle and thread, and a fishing hook and line. More than 10,000 of these easy-to-conceal escape boxes were used by pilots during the war. The escape boxes often were all they had to help them evade capture and make it to safe territory after being shot down.

But as the war continued, Hutton's biggest challenge wasn't inventing his escape tools, or outfitting soldiers and pilots with them before they entered into battle. His biggest challenge was smuggling the escape tools into prison camps to aid in the escapes of British prisoners of war (including ones in Colditz

This British pilot's uniform could be converted into an ordinary suit by turning the jacket inside-out.

Castle, which you read about on page 38). That's because whenever prisoners received packages (including food from the Red Cross), German guards searched through them before passing them on to the prisoners. Hutton had to work doubly hard to make concealments that could pass undetected right under the nose of an enemy guard!

The packages with Hutton's escape aids hidden inside became known as "naughty parcels," and during the war, more than 1,500 of them were sent to prisoner-of-war camps. Since the aids were so well hidden, the prisoners *themselves* had to be

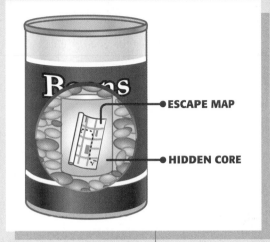

ESCAPE MAP

HIDDEN CORE

given a **coded** message to let them know to look for them. Sometimes the message was hidden in the package label itself. For example, if a prisoner got a package from Mrs. Mappin, it meant there was a "map in" it!

After realizing that prisoners were getting their hands on Hutton's creations, the German guards began to search even more carefully through every parcel. After they found a book cover with a map inside, they ripped all covers from books. They broke all music records to check for maps and money after discovering that records had been

used to smuggle those items into the camp. But Hutton was always one step ahead of them, coming up with more and more clever ways to conceal things.

Hutton slipped compasses into soap and walnuts, buried a screwdriver in a cricket bat, and even concealed a saw in a toothbrush. He produced a Monopoly board game that hid real money, and he convinced the Gillette Company to make razors that concealed compasses. Prisoners received blankets that were coated with a special chemical. When they were washed, a cutout pattern for a civilian overcoat appeared. Once assembled, the overcoat could be worn as a disguise by escaping prisoners.

When Hutton learned that cans of food were being punctured on both sides by guards to make sure there really was food inside, he developed a special can with two layers of metal on each side. If the can was punctured, food spilled out to satisfy the guards. But hidden in the core of the can was an escape map!

At times, Hutton worked on disguising his goods all night long. He even had a special bunker (an underground shelter) built so he could work without being disturbed. Sound a little eccentric to you? Well, even so, his hard work certainly paid off. According to historians, thousands of British soldiers and pilots escaped or evaded capture during World War II. And a large number of them owed their success to the efforts of MI9 and, most of all, to the creative genius of Clayton Hutton.

catch you later!

Catch you later? Well, maybe now we *won't* be able to catch you—especially if you've worked hard to master this month's escape and **evasion** techniques!

You now have the know-how to get to safety with an escape map and kit, to navigate with your compass and the North Star, and even to signal for help using a mirror or a rocket! Plus, you've learned about some great escape tools and some amazing ways to conceal them.

Here's your final challenge for this month. Decode this tapped message to learn the name of one of the greatest escape artists of all time. This "escapologist" dazzled audiences in the early 1900s with amazing feats like escaping from a padlocked iron can filled with water, wriggling out of a straightjacket, and even jumping off a bridge while tied with locks and chains!

Tap, tap, tap. Tap, tap.
Tap, tap, tap, tap. Tap, tap, tap.
Tap, tap, tap, tap, tap. Tap, tap, tap, tap.
Tap, tap, tap, tap. Tap.
Tap, tap, tap, tap. Tap, tap.
Tap, tap, tap. Tap, tap, tap.
Tap, tap, tap, tap. Tap, tap.

48